USS Hornet Museum Explorer Book

Welcome Aboard!

Welcome to the USS *Hornet* Sea, Air & Space Museum! Launched in 1943, the USS *Hornet* has been serving our country for over 80 years. First as a warship during World War II, next in the Cold War in the 1950s and 1960s, then deployed during the Vietnam War in the late 1960s, and finally as part of NASA's Apollo Moon program in 1969! After her retirement, she was put into reserve and then sold for scrap. At the last moment, she was saved and now serves as a museum ship in Alameda, California!

USS *Hornet* CV-12 soon after launch in 1943

What is an Aircraft Carrier?

An Aircraft Carrier is a ship that also carries aircraft. That means it is a ship, a floating airport, and a floating city for its 3,000 crew all at the same time. It has to cross the oceans, carry, arm, launch and land its aircraft. It has to have places for the crew to work, sleep, eat, take showers, get a haircut, visit the dentist, etc. Since the ship can be at sea for weeks at a time, it has to be able to carry everything it needs.

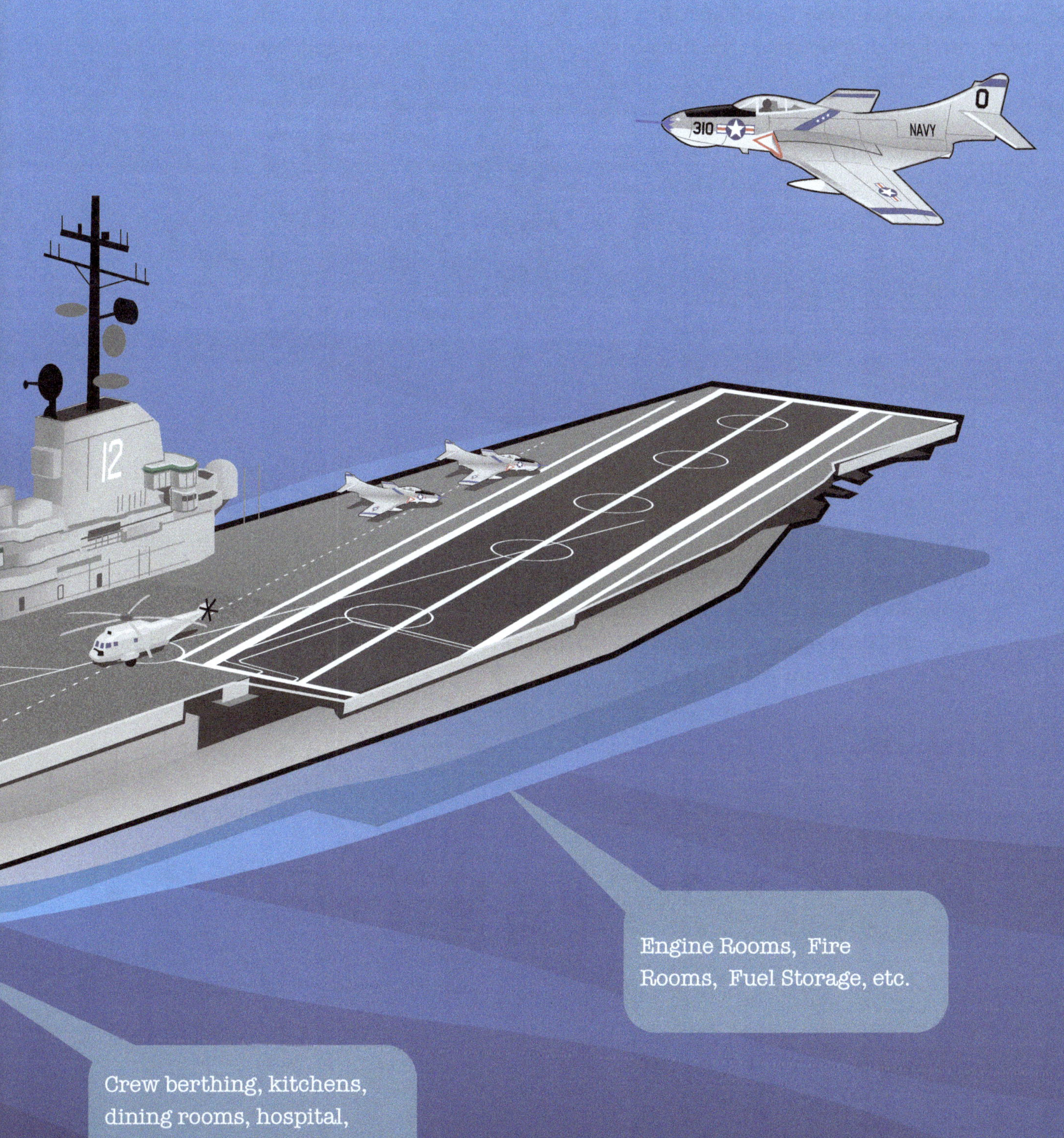
12
310
NAVY
O
Engine Rooms, Fire Rooms, Fuel Storage, etc.
Crew berthing, kitchens, dining rooms, hospital, workshops, etc.

EARLY AVIATION MILESTONES

The Wright Brothers made the first flight in a heavier-than-air craft at Kitty Hawk in North Carolina in 1903. Frenchman Henri Fabre flew the first seaplane in 1910. Eugene Burton Ely was the first person to land a plane on a ship in 1911 in San Francisco Bay.

Wright Brothers Flyer in 1903

Early Aircraft Carriers

The first Seaplane tenders began going into service in 1911, starting with the French ship *Foudre*, followed by the British ship *Hermes*. The US Navy used the battleship USS *Mississippi* as a seaplane tender in 1913. Seaplane tenders were built with cranes and maintenance spaces to carry supplies for the seaplanes and to bring them on and off the ship, although the seaplanes didn't take off from these ships. The Japanese conducted the first naval-launched air raid in 1914 from the *Wakamiya*.

French Seaplane Tender *Foudre*

British Seaplane Tender HMS *Hermes*

United States Seaplane Tender *Mississippi*

Japanese Seaplane Tender *Wakamiya*.

Henri Fabre's seaplane flight in 1910

Eugene Burton Ely's landing on the USS *Pennsylvania* in 1911

HMS *Ark Royal*

The first of what we would consider modern aircraft carriers was the flat deck carrier of the British Navy, the HMS *Ark Royal* (although technically a seaplane tender), specifically built so aircraft could take off and land on the deck. This was followed by the first ship with a full flight deck, the HMS *Argus*, and then the first purpose-built Aircraft Carrier by the Japanese, the IJN *Hosho*.

HMS *Argus*

IJN *Hosho*.

The First US Aircraft Carrier: The USS Langley CV-1

The United States Navy commissioned its first aircraft carrier in 1920 after converting it from a collier (a ship that hauls coal). The letters and numbers after the name have specific meanings in the United States Navy. CV-1 stands for Cruiser (C), Aviation (V), and the "1" means this is the first ship of this type commissioned. The USS *Langley* CV-1 was a very important ship for the Navy as it allowed them to test naval aviation for almost a decade before the next aircraft carrier was completed. This allowed the Navy to incorporate all the lessons learned operating the *Langley*.

CV-1

THE NEXT 7 AIRCRAFT CARRIERS

The *Lexington* Class (USS *Lexington* CV-2, USS *Saratoga* CV-3) were converted battlecruisers to comply with the navy building treaties of the time. They were larger and more heavily armed than other carriers and both entered service in 1928. The USS *Ranger* (CV-4) was a smaller carrier built to fit into tonnage limitations of the time and commissioned in 1934, the only ship of her class.

There were 3 *Yorktown* class carriers, USS *Yorktown* CV-5, USS *Enterprise* CV-6, and USS *Hornet* CV-8. These carriers were larger and incorporated more of what the Navy wanted. They were commissioned just in time for World War II-1937, 1938, and 1941, respectively. The USS *Wasp* CV-7 was another smaller ship, the only one of her class. It started just before the naval treaties ended but was commissioned in 1940. These were the aircraft carriers used to test naval air operations before World War II and were available to the US Navy when the US entered World War II.

USS *Lexington* CV-2

USS *Saratoga* CV-3

USS *Ranger* CV-4

USS *Yorktown* CV-5

USS *Enterprise* CV-6

USS *Wasp* CV-7

USS *Hornet* CV-8

World War II – US Neutrality, Tensions with the Japanese

World War II officially started on September 1st, 1939, when Germany invaded Poland. The United States stayed neutral at first, not wanting to get involved in another European War. In the Pacific, the Japanese had been fighting China since 1937. The United States established a series of trade restrictions on Japan to influence them to stop hostilities with China. After France fell in 1940 to Germany, Japan occupied French Indochina (now Vietnam, Laos, and Cambodia). At this point, the United States set a complete embargo on oil, steel, and other critical resources that Japan's military needed. Japan was now in a difficult position if it wanted to continue its Imperial ambitions.

Map of the Pacific before the Japanese attack on Pearl Harbor

Design of the Essex Class Aircraft Carrier

With the threat of war on the horizon and the large size of the Japanese navy as a major concern, the United States began a large shipbuilding project in 1940. Among all the ships the navy wanted was a new class of aircraft carrier, the *Essex* class. This ship design would incorporate everything learned from the first 8 aircraft carriers. Essentially an upgrade of the *Yorktown* class, the *Essex* class could hold more fuel and ammunition, have a longer range, a better aircraft elevator system, and many other small improvements. The Navy would eventually build 24 of this class of aircraft carrier, more than any other capital ship. The *Essex* class carrier, with radar, lots of anti-aircraft guns, high speed, and an air group that grew to over 100 planes, was to be one of several war-winning weapons of World War II in the Pacific. The first *Essex* class carrier launched was the USS *Essex* CV-9.

USS *Essex* CV-9

Pearl Harbor

Finally, the Japanese empire decided that without oil from the United States, it would have to acquire its oil from the Dutch East Indies (now Indonesia). To do this, they felt they would have to defeat the navies of both Great Britain and the United States. The United States navy posed the larger threat, so the Japanese planned a sneak attack on the main US Navy base in the Pacific, Pearl Harbor. On December 7th, 1941, without declaring war, the Japanese struck Pearl Harbor with aircraft from 6 aircraft carriers. In two air raids, the Japanese inflicted 3,435 casualties and sank 4 battleships, severely damaged 4 more, damaged 3 light cruisers, 3 destroyers, and 3 other ships. Over 188 aircraft were destroyed and another 159 were damaged. The Japanese only lost 5 midget submarines and 29 aircraft shot down, with another 79 damaged. Luckily for the US Navy, none of their aircraft carriers were at Pearl Harbor when it was attacked.

The USS *Shaw* exploding after the attack by Japanese aircraft.

USS West *Virginia* burning during the Pearl Harbor attack

Destroyed US aircraft after Japanese attack.

Early Pacific Battles

The Japanese quickly conquered large parts of the Pacific. However, with their aircraft carriers, the United States found ways to fight back. They launched raids and fought several pitched battles, slowing and eventually stopping the Japanese expansion.

Explosion on USS *Lexington* CV-2 on fire during the Battle of the Coral Sea.

Henderson Field on Guadalcanal

Japanese carrier Shoho hit by a Torpedo
during the Battle of the Coral Sea

B-25s on the USS *Hornet* CV-8 for the
Doolittle Raid

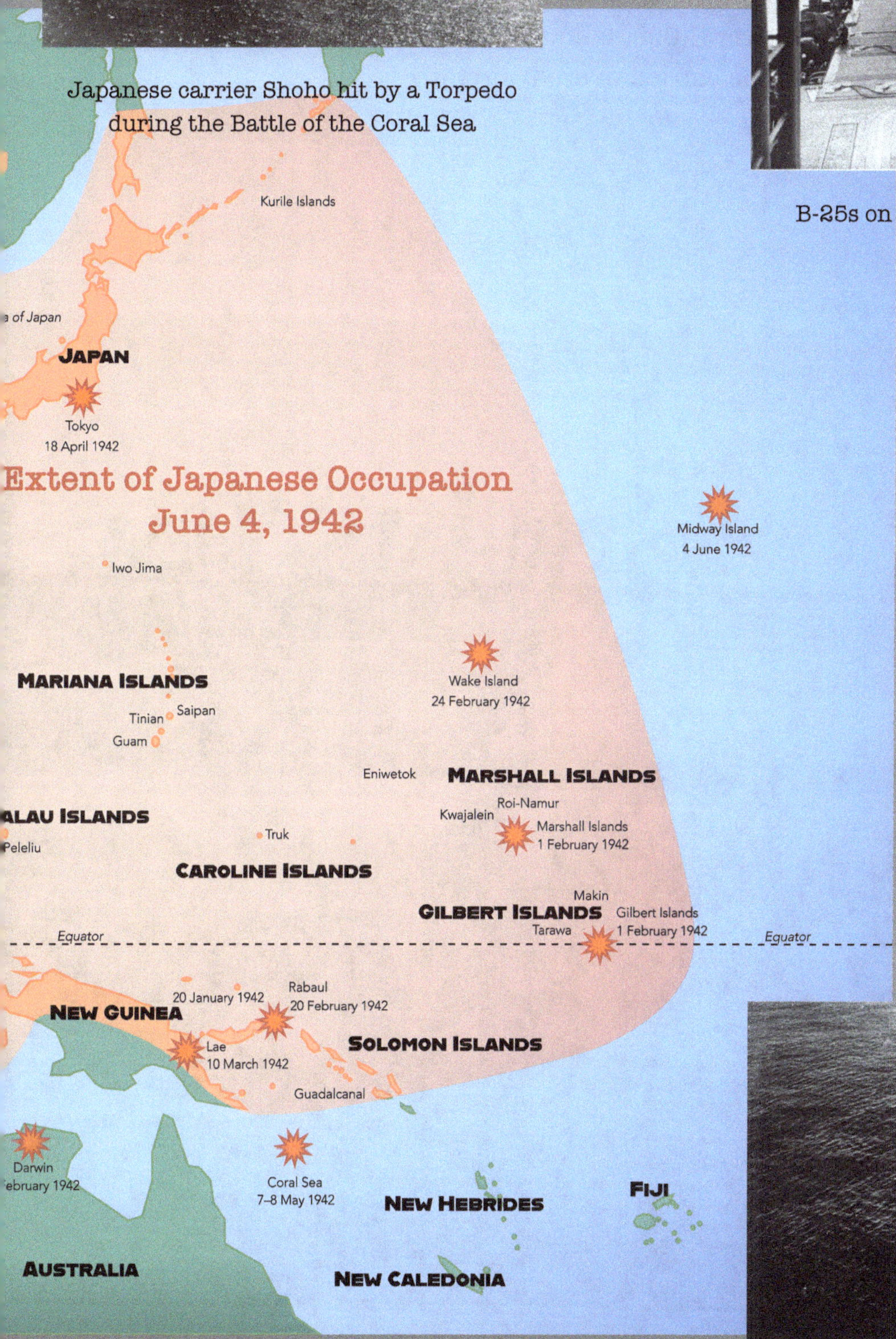

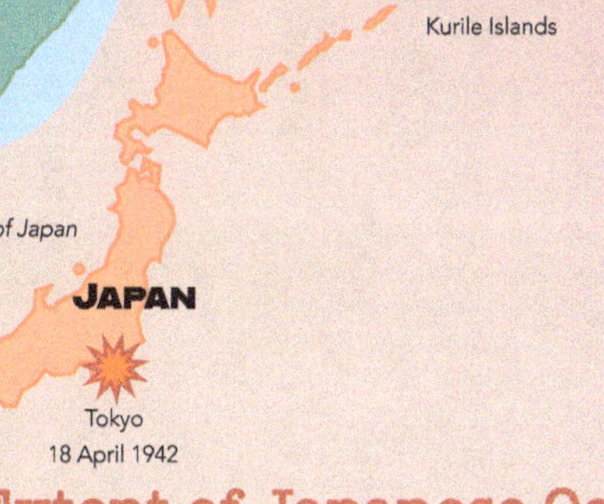

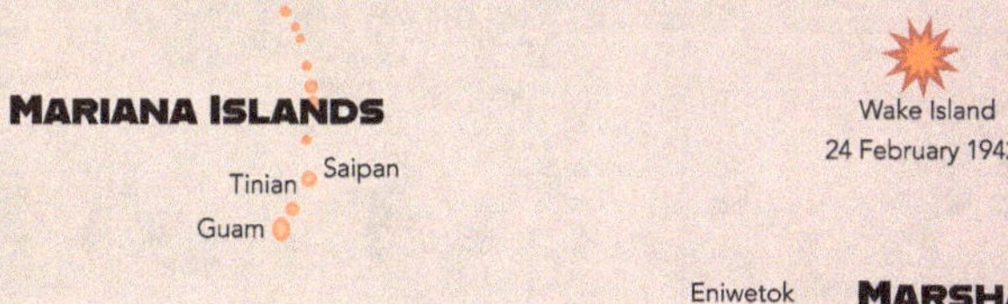

Early battles of World War II in the Pacific.

Japanese carrier Hiryu on fire after attack
by US aircraft.

LAUNCH OF THE USS HORNET CV-12

Construction of the USS *Hornet* started on August 3rd 1942; she was launched on August 30th 1943, and was commissioned into the Navy on November 29th 1943. She conducted her shakedown cruise and then joined the Pacific fleet in February 1944. The USS *Hornet* was almost 900' long and carried over 3,000 sailors, officers and aircrews. Her engines produced 150,000 Horsepower and she carried over 90 aircraft.

Chaplain of the sunken USS *Hornet* CV-8 prepares the christening of the USS *Hornet* CV-12.

Mrs. Knox, wife of the Secretary of the Navy, christens the USS *Hornet* CV-12.

Aircraft Carried by the USS Hornet

The USS *Hornet* carried Hellcat Fighters, Helldiver Dive-Bombers, and Avenger Torpedo Bombers. Their Japanese opponents carried Zeke (also called Zero) Fighters, Judy Dive Bombers, and Jill Torpedo Bombers.

Grumman "Hellcat" Fighter

Curtis "Helldiver" Dive Bomber

Grumman "Avenger" Torpedo Bomber

JAPANESE OPPONENTS

Their Japanese opponents carried Zeke (also called Zero) Fighters, Judy Dive Bombers and Jill Torpedo Bombers.

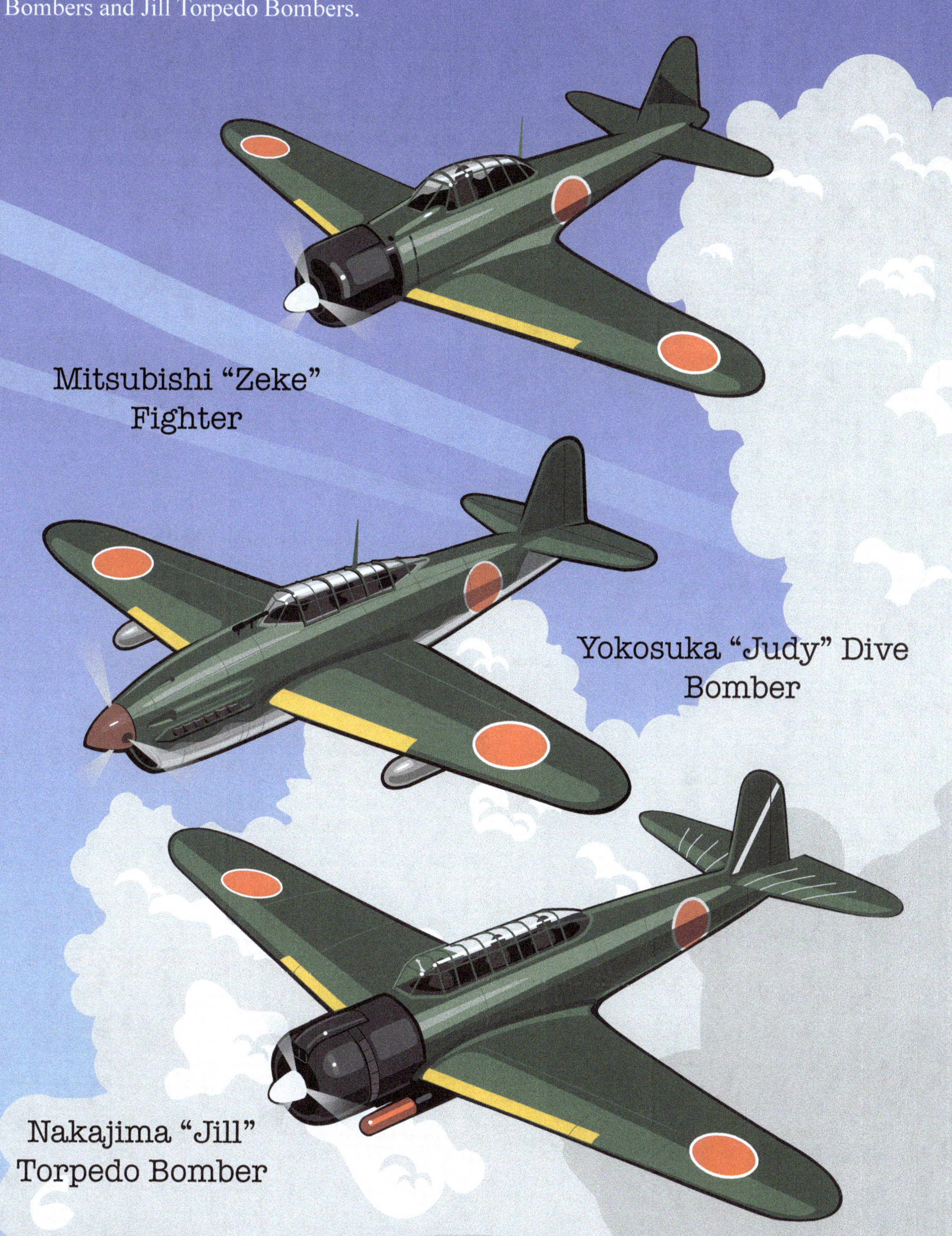

MAJOR BATTLES AND RAIDS

For the next year and three months, the USS *Hornet* served with the Pacific Fleet in almost every major naval battle in the Pacific. Every single battle was a victory as the Japanese forces were pushed back further and further.

Avenger Torpedo Bombers above the
USS *Hornet* CV-12

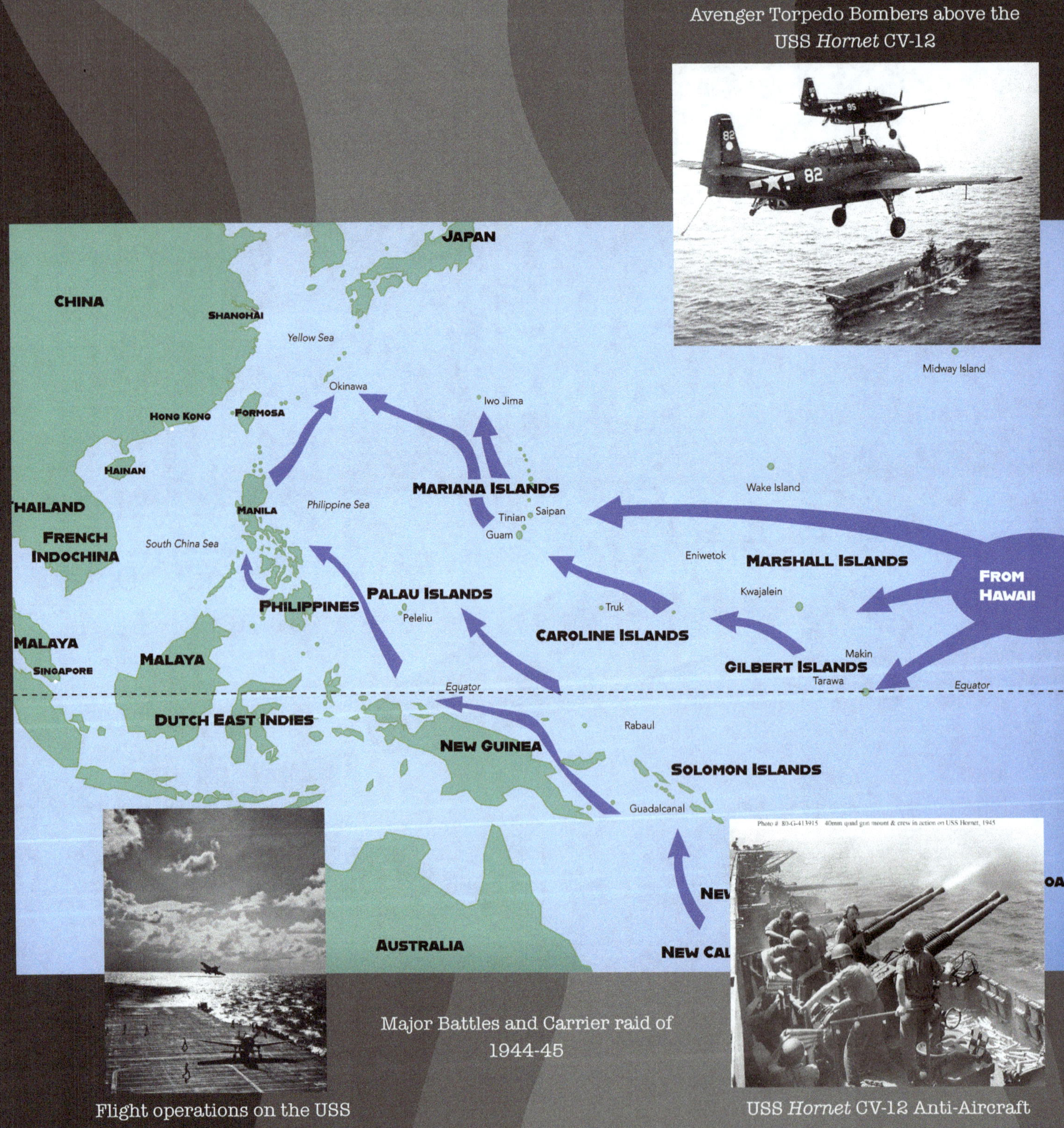

Major Battles and Carrier raid of
1944-45

Flight operations on the USS
Hornet CV-12

USS *Hornet* CV-12 Anti-Aircraft
guns in action

KAMIKAZES

As the war went on, the Japanese began to get desperate. They realized they couldn't match the ever-growing US Navy as their own Navy shrunk. They invented a new weapon to fight back: The Kamikaze. Japanese pilots would deliberately crash their planes into US ships in an attempt to turn the tide of the war. These attacks did cause a lot of damage, but in the end, they weren't enough to stop the US forces.

Rising Sun flag

Kamikazes preparing to take off

USS St. Lo CVE-63 hit by a kamikaze

KNOCKED OUT BY A TYPHOON

In June of 1945, Mother Nature did what no enemy aircraft or ship had been able to do, and that was to cause serious damage to the *Hornet*-to the extent that she was knocked out of the war! While caught in a typhoon in the Pacific Ocean, a giant wave crashed over the bow of the USS *Hornet* and collapsed the front part of the flight deck. This caused the ship to get sent back to San Francisco for repairs, and by the time the repairs were done, the war was over.

Hurricane damage to the flight deck of the USS Horn

OPERATION MAGIC CARPET

After the war ended, the USS *Hornet* was converted into a passenger liner. Thousands of bunks were welded into the hangar bay where planes were normally stored and the USS *Hornet* made 5 trips from the Pacific Islands back to the West Coast of the U.S. with thousands of servicemen aboard.

US servicemen in the hangar bay of the USS *Enterprise* CV-6 during Operation Magic Carpet.

Illustration on a booklet given to US personnel during Operation magic Carpet

Reserve Fleet, Korean War, and Re-fit to Handle Jets

After Operation Magic Carpet, the USS *Hornet* was decommissioned and sent to the reserve fleet. When the Korean War broke out, the US Navy needed to bring many ships back into service, and the USS *Hornet* was sent for modernization. The ship was upgraded to handle jets—many parts of the ship had to be strengthened, more fuel capacity was needed, catapults were modernized to launch the heavier jets, etc. As it turns out, the Korean War was over by the time this was finished, but the USS *Hornet* was put back into service as the CVA-12 (A for "attack").

Aircraft had changed a lot since World War II. The USS *Hornet* now carried Jets and Helicopters in addition to propeller aircraft.

USS *Hornet* CVA-12 after re-fit with the New York skyline in the background in 1953.

Douglas A-1 Skyraiders over the USS *Hornet* CVA-12

McDonnell F2H-3 Banshee

Grumman F9F-6 Cougar

Rescued pilot exiting from a Piasecki HUP-2 Retriever helicopter

AROUND THE WORLD CRUISE

The USS *Hornet* was supposed to join the Pacific Fleet, but the modernization was completed in Virginia, and the US Navy decided to send the ship to the Pacific the long way by going east. The USS *Hornet* crossed the Atlantic Ocean and visited Portugal, Italy, Egypt, Ceylon and then into the Pacific.

USS *Hornet* CVA-12 in the Suez Canal during her around-the-world cruise.

COLD WAR TENSIONS

During the mid-1950s and early 1960s, there were multiple incidents, usually with China, that brought the U.S. 7th fleet into the Western Pacific to make a show of force and prevent full-on war. The main drivers of these conflicts were the desire of the People's Republic of China to reclaim Taiwan and the independence movement in Vietnam. Aircraft Carriers such as the USS *Hornet* were called again and again the project force into these areas.

Incidents in the South China Sea and surrounding areas

ANTI-SUBMARINE CARRIER

In 1958, the USS *Hornet* was upgraded again. As the newer carriers became larger and larger and the threat of Soviet submarines increased, the US Navy found a new role for the old *Essex* class carriers: Submarine hunter. The carrier had sonar equipment added, an increase in the capacity of the combat information center and many other changes made. The air squadrons were also changed dramatically to consist primarily of helicopters and anti-submarine aircraft. Their job was now to protect the newer, larger attack carriers and the waters around US bases by tracking and destroying submarines.

USS *Hornet* CVS-12 with anti-submarine aircraft on deck.

Close up of S-2 loading for a mission.

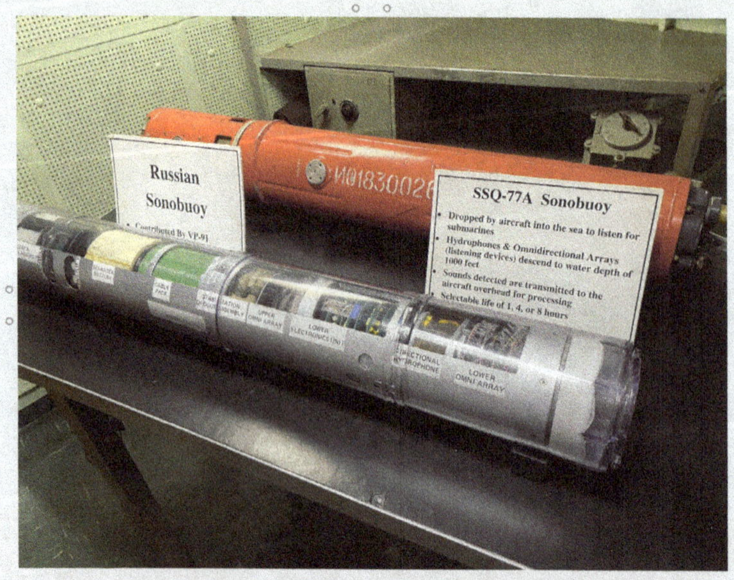

Examples of a U.S. and Soviet Sonar buoy.

ANGLED FLIGHT DECK

A significant change made during a refit in 1958 was the addition of the angled flight deck. This British invention allowed for a significant improvement in flight operations. Aircraft would take off from the front as usual, but landing aircraft landed on the angled part-meaning if they missed the arrestor hook wires, they could simply take off again and circle around for another try.

USS *Hornet* CVS-12 undergoing at sea re-supply showing a good view of the angled flight deck.

AIRCRAFT OF THIS ERA

During this time, the USS *Hornet* aircraft consisted of helicopters, anti-submarine aircraft, and a few attack aircraft. The S-2 Tracker, the A-4 Skyhawk and H-34 Seabat Helicopters were the most well-known. The S-2 was considered a very good aircraft, and it was the first one designed to both find and destroy submarines. Several planes are on display at the USS Hornet Museum.

Douglas TA-J4 Skyhawk on display at the
USS *Hornet* museum.

Grumman US-2B Tracker on display at the
USS *Hornet* museum

Sikorsky UH-34D Seahorse on display at the
USS *Hornet* museum

Vietnam War

The United States began to get involved in the Vietnam conflict in the early 1960s. North Vietnam Was a communist country and South Vietnam was a democratic country. North Vietnam wanted to reunify the country, and the United States was committed to stopping the spread of Communism. As the conflict expanded, the United States became increasingly involved. North Vietnam eventually triumphed after the United States left what was a very unpopular war at home. Vietnam is now one country. The United States Navy was heavily involved in this conflict, with ships stationed off the coast providing support to the ground troops fighting on land. The USS *Hornet* served 3 tours off the coast of North Vietnam at the so-called Yankee Station (the position of Yankee Station changed over time). Her role was mostly patrolling for submarines and search and rescue operations for downed pilots. The other major deployment area was Dixie Station off South Vietnam.

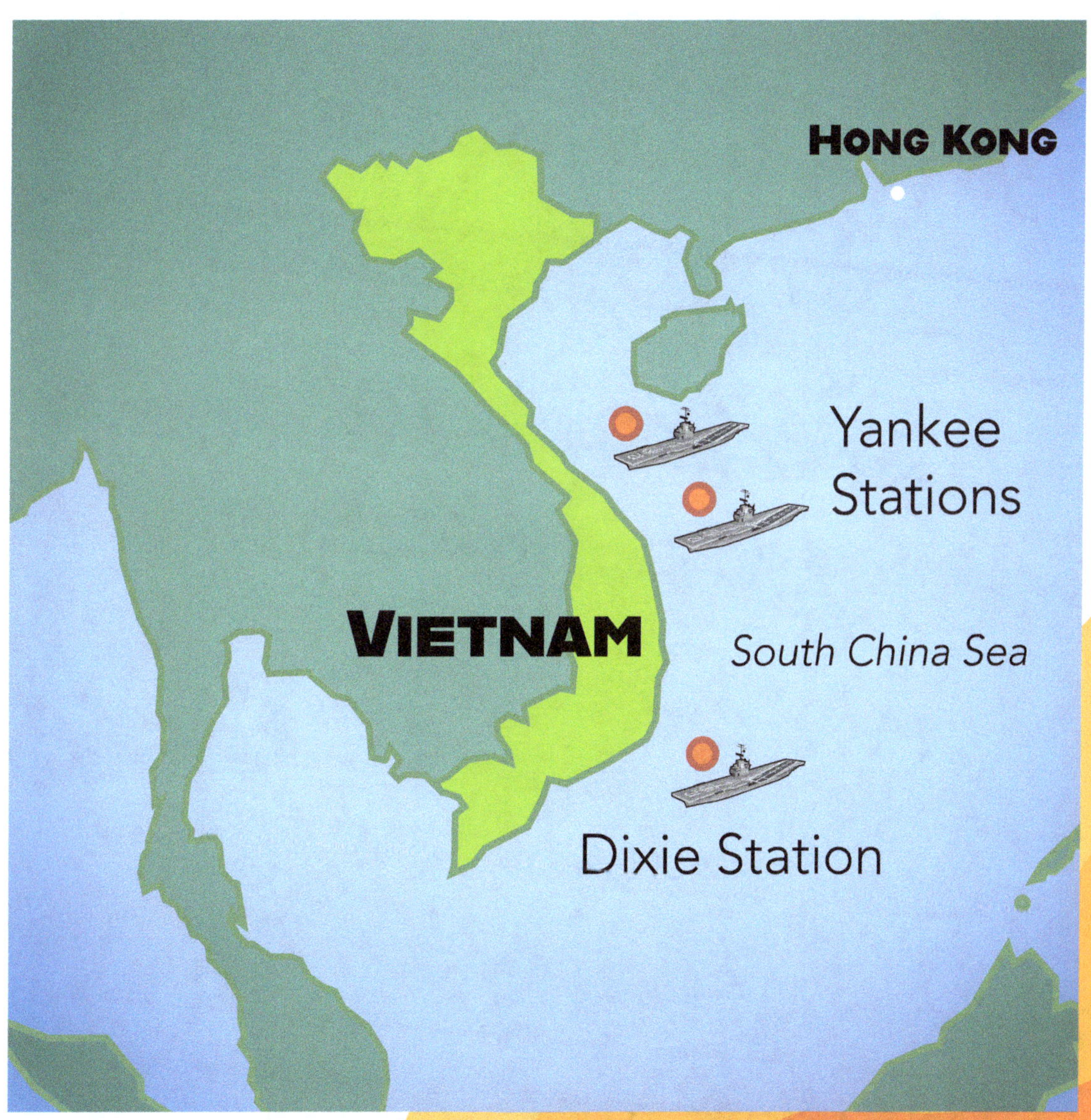

Map of North Vietnam and South Vietnam showing Yankee and Dixie stations.

APOLLO 11

President Kennedy promised that the United States would send astronauts to the Moon and bring them safely back to earth before the end of the 1960s. In 1969, Apollo 11 lifted off with Neil Armstrong, Buzz Aldrin and Michael Collins. Armstrong and Aldrin became the first humans to walk on the Moon on July 20th, 1969 and then all three astronauts returned to Earth. When they splashed down in the Pacific Ocean, the USS *Hornet* was there waiting to pick them up on July 24th 1969. The ship was packed with special equipment, mission specialists, Navy frogmen and even President Nixon. The astronauts were safely recovered and transferred to a mobile quarantine facility (in case they had Moon germs!) and then greeted by President Nixon himself!

Neil Armstrong on the Moon. Photo by NASA.

Lunar Module after lift off from the Moon.
Photo by NASA.

Command module after splashdown with
Navy Divers alongside.

USS *Hornet* CVS-12 about to pick up the
Command Module.

US President Nixon speaking with the
returned astronauts.

Apollo Block 1 Command Module on display at
the USS *Hornet* museum.

Mobile Quarantine Facility (MQF) on display at the
USS *Hornet* museum.

Apollo 12

Apollo 12 was the 2nd mission to the moon and back and included an all navy crew of Pete Conrad, Richard Gordon and Alan Bean. After walking on the moon and returning, they were picked up by the expert crew of the USS *Hornet* on November 24th, 1969. It was another flawless recovery and a testament to the skill of everyone involved.

SeaKing helicopter hovering above the Apollo 12 Command Module as the astronauts exit.

Apollo 12 Mission Patch

USS *Hornet* CVS-12 maneuvering to recover the Apollo 12 Command Module.

USS Hornet Museum

On October 17, 1998, the USS Hornet opened as a museum at Pier 3 of the former Alameda Naval Air Station. Buzz Aldrin from Apollo 11 was the featured speaker. The ship is still at the same pier today. Thousands of people came aboard to celebrate the opening.

RETIREMENT

On June 26th, 1970, the USS *Hornet* retired from Navy service for good. She was "mothballed" at Puget Sound Naval Shipyard and Intermediate Maintenance Facility. She would stay there until the 1990s when she was sold for scrap. Before she could be scrapped, Captain Jim Dodge of the Alameda Naval Air Station borrowed her as part of his closing ceremonies for the base. During this time, she was saved by an organization called the Aircraft Carrier *Hornet* Foundation which successfully argued with the NAVY that the *Hornet* could not be scrapped since she had been designated a historical landmark.

USS *Hornet* CVS-12 at Puget Sound.

Hunter's Point Shipyard in San Francisco

Alameda Naval Air Station before closing

Opening Ceremonies of the USS *Hornet* Museum in 1998.

MUSEUM HIGHLIGHTS-AIRCRAFT

The USS *Hornet* Museum has a great collection of aircraft. From World War II, there is a Grumman F4F Wildcat and a TBM Avenger Torpedo Bomber. From the 1950s, there is an FJ2 Fury. From the 1960s, there has been an F8U-1 Crusader, TA-4J Skyhawk and an S-2 Tracker. From the 1970s there an F-14 Tomcat and an S-3 Viking. The helicopter collection includes a HUP-1 Retriever, an SH-2 Seasprite, and more. All in all, there are over a dozen aircraft in the collection.

Vought F8U-1 Crusader

Grumman FM-2 Wildcat

Sikorsky SH3H SeaKing

F-14A Tomcat

Museum Highlights- Restored Areas

Many areas of the ship are open to the public: All the Hangar Bays, the Flight Deck, the officer's quarters, a ready room, the officer's wardroom, sick bay, laundry room, sailor's berthing areas, the Marine berthing area and much more. Other areas are only accessible on guided tours, such as the engine room, catapult room, navigation bridge, special weapons, and many more areas.

Hangar Bay 2 aircraft refueling station

Combat Information Center

Island structure on the flight deck

Air Squadron Ready Room

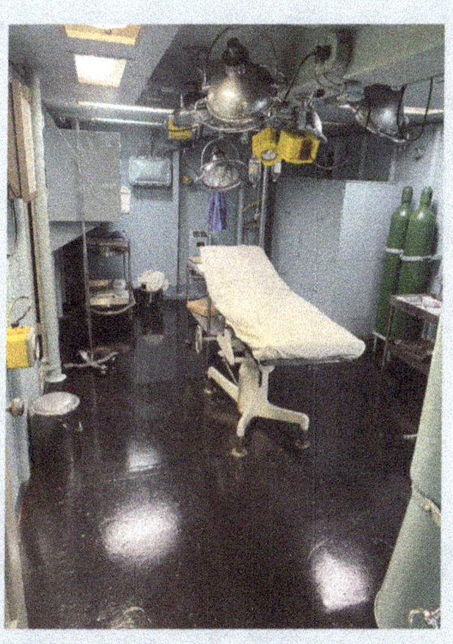

Sick Bay

Friends and Families of Nisei Veterans 442nd Exhibit

African-Americans in the Military Exhibit

MUSEUM HIGHLIGHTS-EXHIBITS

Many rooms in the ship have been turned into exhibits featuring such topics as Women in the military, African Americans In the Military, Air Group 11 from World War II, Anti-Submarine warfare, sister ship row, the 442nd Japanese-American exhibit and others.

Air Group 11 Exhibit

Women in the Military Exhibit

Educational Activities

The USS *Hornet* Museum education department offers many different programs such as Field Trips, Overnights, Remote Presentations, Special Tours and more. The themes include STEM education, the history of the ship, the life of a sailor, pilot's stories, the Apollo space program and many others. Thousands of kids a year enjoy the educational programs of the *Hornet*.

Guests about to onboard for an overnight at the USS *Hornet* museum

Scouts

The USS *Hornet* Museum partners with local scouting organizations on a merit badge program and hosts many field trips and overnight programs for scouts.

Boy Scouts on the USS *Hornet* Museum.

Ghost Hunting

The Grey Ghost (nickname for the USS *Hornet*) is a magnet for those searching for paranormal activities. The ship hosts monthly flashlight ghost hunting tours and overnights. Many paranormal experts come to the *Hornet* to investigate for themselves.

Are there ghosts on the USS *Hornet*? Come aboard and find out!

COMMUNITY EVENTS

Every year, the crew of the *Hornet* holds large community events for our visitors. We have a New Year's Eve party, Halloween Dance Party, CarrierCon (a cosplay event), and the 4th of July celebration, to name a few. We also honor our veterans on Memorial Day, Veterans Day and Vietnam War Veterans Day. We observe the anniversaries of the Apollo 11 and 12 moon missions with space exploration-themed events.

New Year's Eve celebration

Monster's Bash Halloween Part

CarrierCon Cosplay Event

Veterans Day Event

4th of July celebration

Apollo 11 Recovery Anniversary Celebration

Private Events

The USS *Hornet* is one of the largest venues around and can be rented out for private events such as company meetings, concerts, weddings, birthdays, graduations, proms, and more.

Private event utilizing the stage.

Car show on the pier

Utilizing the *Hornet* Museum as a training facility

Banquet set up for a private event.

Utilizing the hangar bay for a private event.

Community Asset

The USS *Hornet* is a community asset. We are a gathering place for veterans, we host PTSD sessions, we give schools an inexpensive field trip option, we host city meetings such as the Mayor's State of the City Speech, and we host other non-profits.

Alameda Mayor Ashcraft giving a speech at the USS *Hornet* Museum.

The Future

The USS *Hornet* continues to restore and open new areas of the ship for visitors to see. We are continually maintaining the ship, its exhibits, and its artifacts. We are constantly looking for new ways to be a part of the community we are housed in. The ship was launched over 80 years ago and has been a museum for over 25 years, and that is just the beginning!

Imaginary Future Aircraft Carrier Design

The Author & Illustrator

Author Russell Moore works as the Director of Events and Communication at the USS *Hornet* Museum. He has always had an interest in military history, especially the Pacific War, starting when he read Great American Fighter Pilots of WWII by Robert D. Loomis as a child. He has had several Second World War articles published in magazines and had his first book, USS *Hornet* CV-12 Service in Peace and War, published in 2023. Moore lives in Dublin, California, with his wife, Wahida.

By day, Illustrator Stephen Locke is a Creative Director in the San Francisco Bay Area and leads a team of creative professionals in the biotech space. By night, he finds time to pursue his passion for airplane and vehicle illustration, long inspired by the stories of Grandpa Locke, who built P-47 Thunderbolts during WWII.